TIME IS A MID-NIGHT SCREAM

PAVEL Z.
TIME IS A MID-NIGHT SCREAM
fragments from the 1990s

translated from the Czech by Marek Tomin

TWISTED SPOON PRESS • PRAGUE

Copyright © 1999 by Pavel Zajíček
Illustrations © 1999 by Pavel Zajíček
Translation copyright © 2005 by Marek Tomin
Copyright © 2005 by Twisted Spoon Press

All rights reserved under International and Pan-American Copyright Conventions. This book, or parts thereof, may not be used or reproduced in any form, except in the context of reviews, without written permission from the publisher.

ISBN 80-86264-26-2

What is there to say? Bits of thought from a time long past, fragments of broken images that flowed through me then, the invisible continuity of the same, one's ordinary life captured by insignificant words. For me, these writings are a path that leads through the modes of being. This is all I can say.

PAVEL Z.

1

darkness at 1/2 7 in the morning
i wake up on the river's other bank
his eyes took long to close
— i would like to touch you — she said
her touch remote like the ocean
and suddenly the sunset and the sky like a painting
the endless chasm
between where i wake
and you fall asleep

the shadow of my head wandering across the wall

2

he was born in P.*
the river the smell of incense
mirrors and candelabras
he was an altar boy
dreaming long
mea culpa mea maxima culpa!
i wrote the tale of 3 cities
a tale of death and silence
a tale of chaos and a tale of celebrations
i burnt the tale i wrote
the morning sun beyond the window
and nothing is as it seems

New York Praha Paris

---

* Prague

3

who can read books of silence
books without thoughts
books never written
without setting without memories
books of emotion

4

on the map of a city grown old
as on the piece of paper I found in the streets
in your eyes that smiled
at the beginning of the journey
i stepped out of the vicious circle
the moment of transition
to utter the ordinary

5

standing
having awoken
to open one's eyes
and to touch
with awe
the details
of creation

6

i'm here for a moment
unprepared, expecting nothing
your convulsions energize me, my love
all your words your hidden curves your passion
the first flowers of spring are waking
the time of awe begins

7

no
how many times i've said no
it will not come again
that time of neither ecstasy
nor sleep
i took the wrong step
but i don't know where
at what point
i cannot return anyway
so i sit here
thankful for any closeness

8

A. G.*
i saw an old man
reading his poetry
in some new york club
his hands shaking
his childlike eyes
at that moment i knew
poetry has meaning
as a token of memory

---

* Allen Ginsberg

9

next to me on the floor
defeats ecstasy nudity
i have come only to withdraw again
soon after
like a page
torn from a book
an immaculate leaf;
there used to be silence here
what it meant i don't know
i met you as an old man
your situation is different now
i'm unable to fathom it
unable to tell the two apart

10

to speak silently
of what you dream
to reveal caverns of beauty
no matter how awkward that sounds
in the time and place where i am
beauty is not in the visible
it always lies just beyond it all
like a shadow
like an echo
silence

11

what comes to my mind:
the colors of trees are slightly different
death in Zurich
films rolling out one after another
full of people and full of loneliness
full of cities and full of silence
the sounds of a new day
the colors of trees are slightly different
than yesterday
beloved autumn

12

a lifetime of searching for one word
one thought one place
attempts at communication
stay silent feel
a lifetime of fascination
alternating with indolence
a lifetime of being playful like a child
stumbling into walls
a lifetime of the same questions without answers
sleep desire awakening light
wind rushing through the morning city

13

any moment now it seems
or just after midnight
the darkness outside
alone in all those battles
i invent a dream
to avoid sleep

14

the sky bright with the flames of night
falling like strange fireballs
setting the ground ablaze
this city lies in the middle of roads
crisscrossing like contradictory words
faces with receding shadows of likeness
give me hope
touch me

15

red blood of white horses
leaping over the void
i throw a shroud over you
so that you will make an imprint

16

already night
summer's growing old
the cold seeping through the windows
i come to you bearing gifts
they are not visible
if you close your eyes they glow

eyes closed my tongue like that of the blind

17

in some state of mind
on the day of such and such
one place or another
the weather chilly
strange fragrances hover in the room
all begins at an indeterminate point

18

a smoldering fire
rekindled by his lips
in the country of dreams and shadows
cathedral towers after a sleepless night
like thorns in his side
something's being born in blossoming gardens

19

2 candles guttering in an old candleholder
Burroughs' words of love
uttered 2 days before his death
ringing in my ears
i call to you across the void!
at night the full moon now morning
2 pigeons on the rooftop opposite
playing love games
2 cigarettes rolled in a rush
as if something were ending
smoked while walking
as if something were beginning

20

incapable of anything
just sketches and drawings
at 3 in the morning the sun shining
and i — who am i
i'm trying to talk to you
and you're falling asleep
i know nothing about you not even what to say
like a child doesn't
the hum of the empty fridge
4 seasons in one moment
time is a mid-night scream

21

i should be able to discern
i could have learnt a lot by now
masses of people with the same question
"why"?
i have never been able to answer
this question
and why not?
echoes the answer

22

the shadow of an angel moved across the wall
i knew him from somewhere
he leapt out of the window
vanishing around the nearest corner
fragrances and silence remained
i no longer understood who is who
in this strange game
a few minutes past midnight
i stain a leaf of paper

23

a pigeon walking
                along the windowsill
watching you with its glassy
                gaze
vertigo!
walls scribbled with symbols
                of lovemaking
your tongue cannot make you understood
you are silent
i'm a passerby

24

all the old and new places
fragments of these places
the view of your cunt
like a face
smiling
in the face of Death

25

. . . and then a long sleep
i thought about you while sleeping
your number on the box of matches
it was cowardly to ask anything of you
the key from the cellar and the squeaky door
the round table i'm sitting at
is covered with old newspapers
with rings from spilt coffee
scraps of news of the world
from a long time ago
everything's different now
at least i hope

26

fascinated by silence fascinated
by what i have touched
i return to one place
and leave another
many tales hidden in one
fascinated by defeat fascinated by awakening
silhouettes of loneliness
with a stiff smile on my face
i should stay silent better keep silent
invented lives
like old walls sprayed with graffiti
the lights of morning burning out
illuminated pages of arcane books
nudity and disappointment
places transformed before one's eyes
unrecognized upon awakening
it's still burning, something's always burning! — you say
i stride through rain washing away my footprints
as in the beginning
the word whose meaning is being lost
i embarked on a senseless journey
as random as casting dice

lights and faces reflected in puddles
i don't know where to turn
fascinated by the echoes of footsteps
and conversations
i don't understand
maybe right now
someone can express it
walking the streets
i note down the day and rain
neon lights and patterns of puddles
old buildings getting older still
i step over small islands of melting snow
in a café full of smoke and shadows i observe
a living theatre
a situation
i withdraw from after a moment

27

forgotten words and lives forgotten
masks and snow covering the forest track
around the bend just up ahead
the merest glimmer of a few towns
a misunderstanding
something you probably don't want to hear
you lean against the wall
and someone asks you why you're silent
"thinking of you" you reply
"there isn't time" someone else tells you
"time isn't" it occurs to you
as homage to something or someone
you repeat your enchantment
wandering is a kind of game
that one day will end
you drain glass after glass
to find the strength to stand up and leave
— this game lasts only a moment —
and the night undresses before your eyes
like a hallucination
you always wanted to experience

28

your shadow on the wall
like the body i desired
butterflies waking mid-winter
the shadow of a vanishing Nymph dancing
you're not here
only a fire burning out
the stigmata of misunderstanding
you tell me about your desire
about not knowing
i don't know either
i'm just shuffling my feet marking time
in a place full of colors and lights
neon phantoms
and you the nameless one
untouchable
— what you cannot touch does not exist — you say

29

time is in everything always
time of awakening and time of catharsis
strangely potent like a fragrance
midnight sounds and distant journeys
where you walk along walls
through a labyrinth of openness
at the crossing
the moment of differentiation
when you say to yourself
whispering
seeing things one way
when you close your eyes
and another way
when you open them
arms outstretched
wind in your eyes
for a moment you're one step ahead

30

delicate like black velvet
she made the voices of bells ring
like the dark or a mask
now black now white
like a riptide like the wind
like a beast like velvet
she made the voices of bells ring
like wings like sleep
like a sketch like a mask
delicate like black velvet

31

many hours ago
like i always imagined
many lives ago
when i opened a door
watching my own shadow
on that strange town square
i light a cigarette
spring blossoms colors of fall
you appear like fury
when i looked for you
all of last night
gin and tonic
and many forgotten dreams
"there's a whore concealed in every woman's heart"
you said
as though stating
the obvious

32

a pointless jumble of words
a scrapheap of contradictions
a jigsaw of slogans
sighs insults curses
prayers
somewhere on a street
that had a name
he thought he could begin
when all bounds had been broken
there was nothing to lose
to say that the moment
is something that lasts

33

october 7 sunday morning
tea and a piece of stale bread
5 years before millennium's end
dreams the cold the reek of genocide
i search for nonexistent cigarettes
scraps of newspaper reports
like phantasmagorical prophecies
2 naked women smiling
on an old postcard
a hat on my head
casting a shadow on the white wall
the way is open

34

6:55 thursday
reflections of sun rays
a cold shower in the morning
after waking from a bizarre dream
the desire to go far away
the sky torn by birds in flight
dogs bounding through the park
barking
i empty myself

35

which way if you don't know where
follow a curve like a rainbow
over all those bridges
burn like a blaze
filled with joy
by something you did
for its own sake silently

36

love is like spring she said
i never saw her again
like snow melting
vanishing in the soil
soaked to the skin
i walk the streets
as if looking for something
the lost thread
or the fragrance of paradise
as in the ancient tale
i'm listening to now

37

to know when to leave
or not leave at all
gather experience in one place
and the silence of stones below
walk down the stairs with head bowed

38

that face wears its mask with pride
you seek horizons
expecting shortcuts
from place to place in the afternoon
and then back again
into this nameless makeshift transience
that face wears its mask
and your face wears its mask

39

love is a gift not an achievement
in the myths of eternal returns, man desires;
on monday i name the days
sunrise
fidelity betrayal
i name Death
loneliness
i'm not going to name the game of life
it has no rules
i name
kindness subtlety

40

stains on the walls
on the walls stains
like lost continents
in the timeless sea
i grab my head
and chuck it out the window

41

time is what you don't know
an unexpected touch
a blinding light
what you cannot see
time is transformation and waiting
time is patience, a smile
time is an unfinished game
time is nakedness

42

sunday afternoon
a week after his death
a friend
his youth
his books
his interrupted journey
never begun

30.7.95

43

in each chamber a different world
in each situation
momentary cathedrals
cathedrals of illusion

44

words halfway through the night
making no sense
are falling stars
whose heat sets
wordless songs
on fire

45

9 gates into the unknown and 9 tales
like the filaments of a spider's web
half-hearted departures
lives half-lived
weakness is a virtue
distant places
like vanishing islands of awe
9 crossroads i crossed
nudity reflected in mirrors
not to express anything too succinctly
and quickly set it ablaze
find a reason why
witness what passes by
4 seasons and points in time
cross a street in New York
and find yourself
on the 5th floor in Vinohrady
look into the fog-clad park
the ruins of an ivory tower
4 seasons in one moment
9 gates from who knows where
which one to walk through?

9 tales intertwined
like 9 lives half-lived
the moon the stars
in some bar around the corner
pagan dances
miracles revelations
dreams in a hotel room
and self-portraits
nine lives half-lived
hung on the walls

9 gates into the unknown
i walked through

46

love priestesses on the street of pearls
throw away their torn panties
and flee from the sun
the shadows of their angels
seeping into the asphalt
in a church nearby
a baptism
Judith Beatrice
sunday morning
prayers bells
the street's perverse masks
peek in and whisper
    — have mercy on us!
whose mercy on whom?
everything is repeated
in multitudes of colors and images

47

    something between a surreal dream
        and Fellini's vision of life
            with ups and downs like a comedy
something's a film something's a Dream
        the morning streets with the fragrance of
            the sun blossoms garbage
you don't even have to ask
            everything's clear apparently
very close to the ground
            found poems
        apocrypha of ecstasy and emotion.
how will what be when and where?
you can't connect it
in the way a wall an ocean and you alone
        it's a cry
a shadow fleeing across the wall
beans and rice for dinner
and then the light of the lamp
and an open book
        who when where and how? you ask
women love poets you say
but i am you
and that's the contradiction

48

life hallucinates on the edge of night
like a painting of the last supper
and in the afternoon while wandering
life hallucinates
like what you can touch
light
life hallucinates in words
using them to trace
circles of futility

49

to touch like the wind
to catch hold of to lift
like the wind to let go to forget
like dust
like the wind

50

a heart of wax
heated by a flame
dripping
on paper

51

give me strength
to see
to discern
to love
give me hope
give me a smile

52

first words
first breath
first touch
first lovemaking
first betrayal
first sunrays
prayers of awakening birds

53

the mercy strike
on the spikes of your breasts
to depart without pride
at the wrong moment
saying to oneself first there's tenderness
but what is the opposite?
the mercy strike
on the spikes of your breasts
snow is melting

54

"really glad to see you"
i said
Zbyněk H.* the poet
didn't recognize me at first
after taking one step closer
"now i recognize you" he said
in streets where faces and names
can be interchanged
"to whom it may serve"
Emily Dickenson
caressed him with the touch of angels
leaving an outline of pollen
around his lips
to set him apart
from the rest of the world
Francis in conversation
with the birds of heaven
i pound a piece of metal
that's my prayer
that's my scream

---

* Zbyněk Hejda: poet, translator, signatory of Charter 77, recipient of the Seifert Prize (1996).

55

the mysteries of the ordinary
to be woken in the dark
by the song of birds
walk through the city
still sleeping
forget a dream
forget love
as in the mysteries
of the ordinary

56

in half-dreams
and half-worlds
in AS IF country
in half-madness
in half-twilight
in the bermuda triangles
of one particular place
someone's asking
and faceless lips
answer

57

we remained motionless
amid no man's land
in expectation of new shadows
and new events

surrounded by a world
whose interconnections
i couldn't fathom
i smoked a cigarette
and discarded it
i stood too long
in one place
and expected that something
would change

58

let me tell you my light
my fractured image
my awe
a rusty sheet of metal
a sign with the names of poems
a fragment of life
left like an imprint
in a place
i passed through

59

to close oneself off for several days
several weeks
several years
to sit
and stare at the wall
to write an indecipherable book
an image of the world

60

the parable of the lost
a dim light in the window opposite
invent words
emotions colors
invent time
situations faces
kindness
a mist of ecstasy above the pavement
mirrors in the windows opposite
in which you can observe
the parable
of the lost

61

boiling water bubbling
the sound of the alarm clock
a cigarette between the lips
none of this is new
a few paintings on the wall
a few shadows
an Underwood typewriter
nothing much has changed
i'm here by accident
could've been somewhere else
someone else
words are the waste
of some life and time
i've waited long here
the city clad in dark and rain
and that other city radiant inside me
like a phantom
that other face of beauty
the candle burning out
the rest cannot be uttered
something's approaching
and i dreamt something

i should talk about it
shout my joy
or contempt?
bow my head
or howl like an animal?
is it in kindness
or in the face
that's silent?

the breaking of bread
the bread of angels

    21:05, August

62

it's blood-red
the bridges i set ablaze
it's your cunt
burning with the color of blood
it's in the sky at dusk
the color of night
the color of blood
it's the fruit you gather
the fruit of what you planted
it's in your eyes at dusk
it's in the sky
it's blood-red

63

it was a short leg of the journey
a tiny fragment a chimera
he had to get through it
to go further
the semblance of movement
kept him going
hoping
this semblance
was a confirmation
that he was

64

round the corner
round the nearest corner
there it was
lying on the ground
in a little pile
crumbled by the rain
the symbol of the world —
human shit

65

the distance between
what a person is
and what a person wants
tends to be like a void
as if side by side
several shadows walked
cast by someone
lost in the paradox
of halls of mirrors

66

i met
Petr K.* on the streets of Prague
his toothless mouth
scarred by time
i asked
whether he still writes sometimes
"not much, sometimes" — he answered
"enough has been said"
i said somewhat foolishly
he was carrying his morning shopping
i was walking to congratulate
my mother on her nameday
it was May 15
tales unuttered
mingled
with a crowd of tourists
the smiles
me and Petr exchanged
were grimaces
and the howls of lonely wolves
Ekelöf

---

* Petr Kabeš (1941-2005): poet, signatory of Charter 77, recipient of the Seifert Prize (1995) and the State Prize for Literature (2003).

67

precise strokes
above her midriff
like a monumental temple
with central domes

68

words on the verge
of extremes and silence
he crosses points
not knowing
whether their meaning
is in being uttered
or in being unutterable
incommunicable
moments capturing
a sound a cry an echo
a heartbeat

69

fog hovering
above the park
there was a slight frost
i thought about time
part dreaming
part awake
i asked myself
what do i really want
i thought about time now
about
how a person moves
from place to place
to return again
feeling something desiring something
going somewhere carrying fire
carrying doubt carrying joy
i thought about time
whether i should stay
or stand up and leave
there was a slight frost
i opened the window
and stripped naked

70

i talk not to be silent
because silence has many meanings
easy to get lost in
the mask of silence is a cry
my world is contradiction
mirrored doppelgängers
mutants

71

i know those feelings well
i speak to you in words
i can't pronounce
words on the knife-edge of subtlety
that i'm beginning not to believe
we didn't take the next step
standing in one place
grit scraping beneath our feet

72

much can be done
many things are possible
2 suns hovering above my head
rustling their wings
herds of them
phantoms the past
what's your view of the world?
based on what experience?
it's 3 in the morning so let's go!
many pairs of eyes
like scattered gemstones
before my eyes
i eavesdrop on your life
a little afraid to tap
my own
i am a promise broken
by unexpected change
several days after creation
it's not in those dreams
there are no images there
nor maps of journeys
only strange parables
and signs

73

you're like dew in the morning park
wet like the sea
salty like the sea
you're like that
the garden where i rove
you're like that
like dew in the morning park
wet like the sea
you're like that

74

i collect garbage on journeys
and i paste it together
into phantasmagorical tales
about cities and people
i dream of
and love
it's a kind of game
invented
before ancient times
one on one
me against myself

75

a letter
from far away
every word a pearl?
birds
lips
sleep soon
something's growing dark
be don't be
careful

76

it began to burn
the seasons transformed
peasant women
on the train he was arriving in
returning from the last century
their hands clutching
prayer books and rosaries
but it was only a deception
like a certain quarter of Paris
like memories
he didn't want to recall
the blanched ostentatious buildings of the City
poetry?
a powerful story
as yet unuttered
an angelic face revealed
sleeping next to him
on the pillow

77

going round in circles
insignificant in itself
anyone can do it
your head's buzzing
like every night
sunrays stabbing your eyes in the morning
that game of chance is easier
than it seemed
a choice between nudity and covering up
between either and or
with wonder i watch the shapes
of the sky in flux

78

in everything
you cast away
an imprint of your face
like a radiant scar
in all that waste
in every step and glance
a repetition of the imprint
a raw cry
to purge yourself
to stay free
of time and longing

79

pencil marks on paper
a jumble of lines and cries
on the bank of one and the same river
i cover my tracks
in the dew in the morning grass
i cover my tracks
when rawness strikes
i cover my tracks
along walls
i cover my tracks
on the bank of one and the same river
near the sea
i attempt sobriety
and you're asleep . . .

on the bank of one
and the same river
you wake
from your dreams

ABOUT THE AUTHOR

Pavel Zajíček was born in Prague in 1951. During the 1970s he and his experimental band DG307 were part of the unofficial cultural underground that was severly persecuted by Czechoslovakia's communist regime. In 1976 he was sentenced to a year in prison, along with members of The Plastic People of the Universe, for "disturbing the peace," after having been initially charged with "state subversion," which the authorities had to back away from after receiving worldwide condemnation. This trial provided the impetus for the emergence of the human rights declaration and movement Charter 77. Exiled in 1980, Pavel Z. lived in Sweden, where he took citizenship, and then New York City for several years before returning to Prague in the mid-1990s. He continues to play and record with DG307 and has had a number of volumes of his poetry and prose published over the past decade.

ABOUT THE TRANSLATOR

Marek Tomin was born in Prague and grew up in England, where his family found refuge after being exiled in 1980 by the communist regime. After finishing his degree at Oxford University, he returned to Prague in 1992, where he is based today, working as a freelance translator and interpreter, journalist (*Respekt, MF Dnes, Lidové noviny, Czech Business Weekly*), and documentary producer and director (BBC, Czech Television). Closely involved with Greenpeace, Tomin has sailed the Atlantic on numerous occasions.

TIME IS A MID-NIGHT SCREAM
by Pavel Z.

Translated by Marek Tomin

Originally published in Czech as *Čas je výkřik uprostřed noci*
(Prague: MAŤA, 1999)

Illustrations by Pavel Z.
Design by Dr. Pookie
Set in Janson

This is a special edition of 400 copies
published in 2005 by
TWISTED SPOON PRESS
P.O. Box 21—Preslova 12, 150 21 Prague 5, Czech Republic
info@twistedspoon.com / www.twistedspoon.com

Printed and bound in the Czech Republic
by Dragon Press, Klatovy